HOW TO HANDLE KIDS WITH AUTISM (ASD): The Master Guide On Parenting And Teaching Autismic Kids

By

Queen Morbis

Table of content

chapter one
Chapter two
Chapter three
Chapter four
Chapter five

Chapter one

Overview of Autism

Chemical imbalance range jumble (ASD) is a neurological and formative problem that influences how individuals interface with others, convey, learn, and act. Despite the fact that mental imbalance can be analyzed at whatever stage in life, it is depicted as a "formative confusion" since side effects by and large show up in the initial two years of life.

The problem likewise incorporates restricted and redundant examples of conduct. The expression "range" in chemical imbalance range jumble alludes to a large number of side effects and seriousness.

Individuals of all sexes, races, identities and financial foundations can be determined to have ASD. Despite the fact that ASD can be a long-lasting issue, medicines and administrations can work on an individual's side effects and day-to-day working. The American Academy of Pediatrics suggests that all kids get evaluated for mental imbalance. Parental figures ought to converse with their kid's medical services supplier about ASD screening or assessment

Mental imbalance range jumble starts in youth and in the end, creates issues working in the public eye — socially, in school, and at work, for instance. Frequently kids show side effects of mental imbalance inside the main year. Few youngsters seem to foster typically in the main year, and afterward, go through a time of relapse somewhere in the range of 18 and two years old enough when they foster chemical imbalance side effects.

While there is no remedy for mental imbalance range jumble, serious, early treatment can have a major effect on the existence of numerous kids.
Chemical imbalance is portrayed by troubles with neurotypical social cooperation and correspondence; and an inclination to self-manage through redundancy and routine (i.e., extraordinary interests and limited, generalized, and monotonous way of behaving).

Mental imbalance is the quickest developing formative condition, and pervasiveness rates are around 2.8 % (among youngsters 3-17) (National Survey of Children's Health).

Chapter two

The Similarities and Differences Between ADHD And Autism

Regularly individuals struggle with telling whether a youngster has a tad of a meandering consideration, or whether their kid's way of behaving is a mark of a basic condition. Be that as it may, what should guardians examine with experts? Frequently individuals promptly expect it very well may be ADHD or maybe it's an indication of mental imbalance. Some of the time guardians and families struggle with knowing between the two and individuals are generally off track to accept that the two are both on the range. While ADHD and chemical imbalance (Autism) share a ton of comparative characteristics, there are various things that are extraordinary to each condition. Guardians and watchmen need to comprehend the distinctions and likenesses to arrive at the most educated conclusion about their youngsters.

What Is ADHD?

Consideration Deficit Hyperactivity Disorder (ADHD) is a neurodevelopmental problem that influences some places close to 8.5% of youngsters and 2.5% of grown-ups. A condition is described by challenges with consideration, drive control, and hyperactivity. Individuals with ADHD might experience difficulty focusing on the job needing to be done, staying still, or thinking prior to settling on a speedy choice. ADHD influences the way that the cerebrum develops and creates. For the majority, the side effects of ADHD can work on as a youngster develops and acquires concentration or control.

What Is Autism?

Chemical imbalance or Autism Spectrum Disorder can be a particular or a progression of formative problems that influence language abilities, conduct, social connections, coordinated movements, and the capacity to learn. Chemical imbalance influences are somewhere close to 1 out of 59 and 1 of every 65 children. Chemical imbalance causes are as yet not known and there is no conventional "fix" for mental imbalance. Rather, many backers see mental imbalance as a particular piece in a neurodiversity puzzle. Chemical imbalance capabilities range from gentle to serious with various in the middle between.

On a social level, a portion of the battles for youngsters with mental imbalance shows up basically the same as those with ADHD.

The Similarities

Certain parts of both mental imbalance and ADHD cross over and may have all the earmarks of being either. Tragically many children with mental imbalance end up misdiagnosed as having ADHD, yet very few children with ADHD experience something similar. The two circumstances can have restricted social comprehension of their ways of behaving and the impact on others. Individuals with either condition might seem to experience difficulty with focusing on specific things, despite the fact that individuals with ADHD have totally different involvement in their consideration. In general, they have side effects that seem, by all accounts, to be comparable, yet can be radically divergent in specific perspectives.

The Major Differences

There are a few unmistakable variables that are clear lines among mental imbalance and ADHD, in spite of the fact that there are certain individuals that can have both ADHD and chemical imbalance, so guardians and gatekeepers need to perceive the critical contrasts to assist experts with their determination. While both could battle with consideration, individuals with ADHD struggle when requested to focus on a solitary errand, so they will more often than not stay away from undertakings that require fixation. In the meantime, a youngster with mental imbalance could remain hyper-zeroed in on a point that intrigues them, while exhibiting inconvenience in focusing or even give indications of uneasiness when requested to focus on things they're not keen on. Messes with ADHD could talk rapidly and uproariously, needing to triumph ultimately the final word or the principal word in a discussion, while jokes with chemical imbalance might experience issues communicating feelings or considerations verbally. Moreover, they might stay away from the eye-to-eye connection and get social cooperation wrong.

Types Autism

Asperger's condition:
Asperger's condition was the term utilized before 2013, yet presently it has been renamed level I ASD

by the Diagnostic and Statistical Manual of Mental Disorders, Fifth Edition.

Youngsters with Asperger's disorder can speak with others and perform well in school, yet they experience issues socially associating with others. Their way of behaving and figured examples can be rigid and tedious.

Side effects of Asperger's disorder might include:

May invest a ton of energy thinking and discussing one theme or enthusiasm or may just wish to seek after a set number of exercises

The battle to get a handle on group environments as far as correspondence like non-verbal communication, looks, motions, humor, and mockery

Have fewer looks than others

Side interests can become fanatical and disrupt their day-to-day living

Become bothered by even little varieties in their daily schedule

Effectively recall picked data and realities

Trouble controlling feelings, which can prompt verbal or social explosions, self-damaging activities, or fits

Rett condition:

Rett condition is a sort of ASD that influences 1 in every 10,000 ladies and seldom influences men. It is in many cases analyzed in kids matured 6 to year and a half when they start to bomb formative achievements or lose recently gained capacities.

Numerous specialists presently trust Rett disorder to be essential for an illness range brought about by changes in the MECP2 quality, in which there is duplication of the MECP2 quality on the X chromosome.

The rest disorder causes serious shortages in pretty much every component of a youngster's life.

Side effects of Rett's condition might include:

Loss of portability or stride anomalies

Decreased muscle tone

Microcephaly (more modest head size)

Discourse debilitation

Hands lose their usefulness

Compulsory hand developments

Seizures

Trouble relaxing

Dozing issues

Scoliosis (unusual shape of the spine)

Adolescence disintegrative confusion (CDD):

CDD is an uncommon condition that was converged into ASD in the Diagnostic and Statistical Manual of Mental Disorders, Fifth Edition.

The beginning of CDD varies from one individual to another, yet for the most part, it is seen following three years old. Because of its late beginning, there will be a deficiency of recently acquired abilities in friendly, verbal, and engine (connected with development) working in the youngster.

Albeit the specific reason for beginning is obscure, some accept that the condition is a sort of experience growing up with dementia brought about by the development of amyloid (a kind of protein) in the mind. In any case, there is no proof to demonstrate the contention.

Subsequent to showing ordinary improvement for a long time, the youngster might advance into CDD. This happens for the most part somewhere in the range of three and four years, however, may happen any time before 10 years old.

The beginning of CDD might be unexpected or progressive.

Kids might know about the condition and ask what's going on with them.

Guardians or experts may not see formative changes like language, correspondence, social collaborations, and close-to-home turn of events.

Kids might report mind flights (seeing, hearing, or smelling what isn't there).

A youngster who could convey in a few sentences might quit talking steadily.

A youngster who got a kick out of the chance to nestle may totally go against actual contact.

The kid might lose somewhere around two of the accompanying procured abilities:

Engine capacities

Playing skills

Social and taking care of oneself capacities

Expressive language abilities

Open language abilities

Control of the insides or bladder

The youngster might have an unusual capability in no less than two of the accompanying:

Correspondence

Social connection

Dull interests or ways of behaving

Kanner's condition:

Kanner's condition is additionally alluded to as an exemplary mentally unbalanced jumble.

Kids with Kanner's condition will seem brilliant, mindful, and smart, with the problem's basic characteristics, for example,

Failure to shape close-to-home connections with individuals

Wild discourse

Fixation on taking care of items

Correspondence and relational challenges

An elevated degree of repetition memory and visuospatial abilities with huge mastering issues in different regions

Inescapable formative problem not in any case determined (PDD-NOS):

At the point when a youngster with learning and social challenges doesn't satisfy every one of the indicative rules for a specific class of chemical imbalance, then the determination caused will be to be PDD-NOS.

PDD-NOS was the finding given to individuals who fit into this gathering and were remembered to have milder side effects than those with ASD.

Side effects of PDD-NOS might include:

Strange social way of behaving

Inappropriate improvement of abilities like engine, tactile, visual-spatial hierarchical, mental, social, scholastic, and conduct

Correspondence issues

Immature discourse and language abilities

Constant and redundant activities, for example, opening and shutting entryways over and over

Unusual aversion to taste, sight, sound, smell, or potentially contact

Early side effects, reasons for Autism, and Diagnosis

Side effects

A few kids give indications of chemical imbalance range jumble in early earliest stages, for example, decreased eye-to-eye connection, absence of reaction to their name, or lack of concern to guardians. Different kids might grow regularly for the initial not many months or long periods of life, however at that point abruptly become removed or forceful or lose language abilities they've previously gained. Signs as a rule are seen by age 2 years.

Every kid with a mental imbalance range jumble is probably going to have a one-of-a-kind example of conduct and level of seriousness — from low working to advanced.

A few youngsters with mental imbalance range jumble experience issues learning, and some have indications of lower than typical insight. Different youngsters with the problem have typical to high insight — they advance rapidly, yet experience difficulty imparting and applying what they know in day-to-day existence and acclimating to social circumstances.

As a result of the remarkable combination of side effects in every youngster, seriousness can once in a while be hard to decide. It's by and large in view of the degree of hindrances and what they mean for the capacity to work.

Chapter three

Early signs, causes, and Diagnosis of Autism

Social correspondence and cooperation
A youngster or grown-up with mental imbalance range confusion might generally disapprove of social collaboration and relational abilities, including any of these signs:

Neglects to answer their name or seems not to hear you on occasion
Opposes nestling and holding, and appears to favor playing alone, withdrawing into their own reality
Has unfortunate eye-to-eye connection and needs look
Doesn't talk or has postponed discourse, or loses past capacity to say words or sentences
Can't begin a discussion or make a big difference for one, or just begin one to make demands or mark things
Talks with a strange tone or cadence and may utilize a dull voice or robot-like discourse

Rehashes words or expressions word for word yet doesn't have the foggiest idea how to utilize them

Doesn't seem to figure out basic inquiries or bearings

Doesn't liaise feelings or way of thinking and appears untaught about others sentiments

Doesn't show or take an objects to share an attentiveness

Improperly moves toward social cooperation by being inactive, forceful, or troublesome

Experiences issues perceiving nonverbal prompts, for example, deciphering others' looks, body stances, or manner of speaking

Examples of conduct

A youngster or grown-up with mental imbalance range turmoil might have restricted, monotonous examples of conduct, interests, or exercises, including any of these signs:

Performs dull developments, for example, shaking, turning, or hand fluttering

Performs exercises that could inflict any kind of damage, for example, gnawing or head-banging

Creates explicit schedules or customs and ends up being upset at the smallest change

Disapproves of coordination or has odd development designs, like ungainliness or strolling on toes, and has odd, solid, or misrepresented non-verbal communication

Is entranced by the subtleties of an item, for example, the turning wheels of a toy vehicle yet doesn't grasp the general reason or capability of the article

Is surprisingly delicate to light, sound, or contact, yet might be apathetic regarding agony or temperature

Doesn't take part in imitative or pretend play

Focuses on an item or action with strange force or concentration

Has explicit food inclinations, like eating a couple of food sources, or declining food varieties with a specific surface

As they experienced, a few kids with mental imbalance range jumble become more drawn in with others and show fewer aggravations in conduct. Some, generally those with the most unserious issues, in the end, might have typical or close typical existences. Others, in any case, keep on experiencing issues with language or interactive abilities, and the young years can bring more awful social and profound issues.

Children create at their own speed, and many don't follow precise courses of events found in some nurturing books. Yet, youngsters with chemical imbalance range jumble for the most part give a few indications of postponed improvement before age 2 years.

Assuming you're worried about your kid's turn of events or you suspect that your kid might have chemical imbalance range jumble, examine your interests with your primary care physician. The side effects related with the issue can likewise be connected with other formative problems.

Indications of chemical imbalance range jumble frequently show up right off the bat being developed when there are clear postpones in language abilities and social associations. Your PCP might prescribe formative tests to recognize assuming that your kid has delays in mental, language, and interactive abilities, if your kid:

Doesn't answer cheerfully or blissful articulation by a half year
Doesn't emulate sounds or looks by 9 months
Doesn't jibber jabber or coo by a year

Doesn't motion — like point or wave — by 14 months

Doesn't utter a single word for about 16 months

Doesn't play "pretend" or imagine by a year and a half

Doesn't say two-word phrases for two years

Loses language abilities or interactive abilities at whatever stage in life

Causes

Chemical imbalance range jumble has no single known cause. Given the intricacy of the issue, and the way that side effects and seriousness shift, there are most likely many causes. Both inborn or genetic factors and meteorological factors might assume a part.

Inborn factors

A few distinct qualities give off an impression of being engaged with a mental imbalance range jumble. For certain kids, chemical imbalance range confusion can be related to a hereditary problem, like Rett disorder or delicate X condition. For different youngsters, hereditary changes (transformations) may expand the gamble of chemical imbalance range jumble. Then again different qualities might influence mind advancement or the way that synapses convey, or they might decide the seriousness of side effects. A few hereditary changes appear to be acquired, while others happen precipitously.

Meteorological factors

Scientists are at present investigating whether factors like viral diseases, drugs or confusions during pregnancy, or air contaminants assume a part in setting off mental imbalance range jumble.

Diagnosis

Medical care suppliers analyze ASD by assessing an individual's way of behaving and improvement. ASD can for the most part be dependably analyzed by the age of two. Looking for an assessment as quickly as time permits is significant. The prior ASD is analyzed, the sooner medicines and administrations can start.

Analysis of Young Children

Determination in small kids is much of the time a two-stage process.

Stage 1: General Advancing Screening During Well-Child Analysis.

Each kid ought to get well-kid check-ups with a pediatrician or a youth medical care supplier. The American Academy of Pediatrics suggests that all youngsters get evaluated for formative postponements at their 9-, 18-, and 24-or 30-month well-child visits, with explicit chemical imbalance screenings at their 18-and two-year well-child visits. A kid might get extra screening on the off chance that they are at a high gamble for ASD or formative issues. Kids at high gamble incorporate the people who have a relative with ASD, show a few ways of behaving that are common in ASD, have more seasoned guardians, have specific genetic situation, or who had an exceedingly low birth weight.

Taking into account parental figures' encounters and concerns is a significant piece of the evaluating system for small kids. The medical services supplier might pose inquiries about the kid's ways of behaving and assess those responses in blend with data from ASD screening apparatuses and clinical perceptions of the kid. Peruse more about evaluating instruments on the Centers for Disease Control and Prevention (CDC) site.

In the event that a kid shows formative contrasts in conduct or working during this screening system, the medical care supplier might allude the youngster for extra assessment.

Stage 2: Additional Diagnostic Evaluation

It is vital to precisely distinguish and determine kids to have ASD as soon as could be expected, as this will reveal insight into their extraordinary assets and difficulties. Early location additionally can assist guardians with figuring out which administrations, instructive projects, and conduct treatments are probably going to be useful for their youngster.

A set of medical services suppliers who are acquainted with diagnosing ASD will direct the indicative assessment. This group might incorporate youngster nervous system specialists, formative pediatricians, discourse language pathologists, kid analysts and specialists, instructive subject matter experts, and word related advisors.

The symptomatic assessment is probably going to include:

Clinical and neurological assessments
Evaluation of the youngster's mental capacities
Evaluation of the youngster's language capacities
Perception of the youngster's way of behaving
An inside and out discussion with the youngster's guardians about the kid's way of behaving and improvement.
Evaluation of old enough fitting abilities expected to finish day-to-day exercises freely, like eating, dressing, and toileting
Since ASD is a perplexing problem that occasionally happens with different diseases or learning issues, the exhaustive assessment might include:

Blood tests
Hearing test
The result of the assessment might bring about conventional findings and suggestions for treatment.

Conclusion in more established kids and young people

Parental figures and educators are in many cases the first to perceive ASD side effects in quite a while and youths who go to class. The school's practice curriculum group may play out an underlying assessment and later on suggest that a youngster go through extra assessment with their essential medical services supplier or a medical care supplier who have some expertise in ASD.

A kid's parental figures might talk with these medical services suppliers about their kid's social troubles, incorporating issues with inconspicuous correspondence. These unpretentious correspondence contrasts might incorporate issues figuring out manner of speaking, looks, or non-verbal communication. More seasoned youngsters and teenagers might experience difficulty grasping metaphors, humor, or mockery. They likewise may experience difficulty framing fellowships with peers.

Treatment strategies

Current medicines for chemical imbalance range jumble (ASD) try to decrease side effects that impede day to day working and nature of life.1 ASD influences every individual in an unexpected way, implying that individuals with ASD have remarkable qualities and difficulties and different treatment needs.1 Therefore, treatment designs for the most part include various experts and are catered toward the person.

Medicines can be given in schooling, wellbeing, local area, or home settings, or a mix of settings. Suppliers must speak with one another and the individual with ASD and their family to guarantee that treatment objectives and progress are living up to assumptions.

As people with ASD exit from secondary school and develop into adulthood, extra administrations can assist with further developing wellbeing and everyday working, and work with social and local area commitment. As far as some might be concerned, supports to proceed with instruction, complete work preparing, track down business, and secure lodging and transportation might be required.

Kinds of Treatments

There are many kinds of medicines accessible. These medicines by and large can be separated into the accompanying classifications, albeit a few medicines include more than one methodology:

Social
Formative
Instructive
Social-Relational
Pharmacological
Mental
Integral and Alternative

Social Approaches

Social methodologies center around changing ways of behaving by understanding what occurs when the way of behaving. Social methodologies have the most proof for treating the side effects of ASD. They have become generally acknowledged among teachers and medical care experts and are utilized in many schools and therapy centers. An outstanding social treatment for individuals with ASD is called Applied Behavior Analysis (ABA). ABA empowers wanted ways of behaving and deters undesired ways of behaving to work on different abilities. Progress is followed and estimated.

Two ABA showing styles are Discrete Trial Training (DTT) and Pivotal Response Training (PRT).

DTT utilizes bit-by-bit directions to show an ideal way of behaving or reacting. Illustrations are separated into their least difficult aspects and wanted answers and ways of behaving are compensated. Undesired responses and ways of behaving are overlooked.

PRT happens in a characteristic setting as opposed to a facility setting. The objective of PRT is to work on a couple of "essential abilities" that will assist the individual with mastering numerous different abilities. One illustration of vital expertise is to start correspondence with others.

Formative Approaches

Formative methodologies center around working on unambiguous formative abilities, like language abilities or actual abilities, or a more extensive scope of interconnected formative capacities. Formative methodologies are frequently joined with conduct draws near.

The most well-known formative treatment for individuals with ASD is Speech and Language Therapy. Discourse and Language Therapy assists with further developing the individual's comprehension and utilization of discourse and language. Certain individuals with ASD convey verbally. Others might convey using signs, signals, pictures, or an electronic specialized gadget.

Word related Therapy instructs abilities that assist the individual with living as autonomously as could really be expected. Abilities might incorporate dressing, eating, washing, and connecting with individuals. Word-related treatment can likewise include:

Tactile Integration Therapy to assist with further developing reactions to tangible info that might be prohibitive or overpowering.

Non-intrusive treatment can assist with working on actual abilities, like fine developments of the fingers or bigger developments of the storage compartment and body.

The Early Start Denver Model (ESDM) is an expansive formative methodology in view of the standards of Applied Behavior Analysis. It is utilized with youngsters 12 four years old enough.

Guardians and advisors use play, social trades, and shared consideration in normal settings to further develop language, social, and mastering abilities.

Instructive Approaches

Instructive medicines are given in a homeroom setting. One kind of instructive methodology is the Treatment and Education of Autistic and Related Communication-Handicapped Children (TEACCH) approach. TEACCH depends on the possibility that individuals with mental imbalance flourish with consistency and visual learning. It gives instructors ways of changing the study hall structure and work on intellectual and different results. For instance, everyday schedules can be composed or drawn and put in clear sight. Limits can be set around learning stations. Verbal guidelines can be praised with visual directions or actual showings.

Social-Relational Approaches

Social medicines center around working on interactive abilities and building close-to-home bonds. A few social methodologies include guardians or friend coaches.

The Developmental, Individual Differences, Relationship-Based model (additionally called

"Floor time") urges guardians and advisors to follow the interests of the person to grow potential open doors for correspondence.
The Relationship Development Intervention (RDI) model includes exercises that increment inspiration, interest, and capacities to partake in shared social connections.
Social Stories give straightforward portrayals of what's in store in a social circumstance.
Interactive abilities Groups furnish valuable open doors for individuals with ASD to rehearse interactive abilities in an organized climate.

Pharmacological Approaches

There are no drugs that treat the center side effects of ASD. A few drugs treat co-happening side effects that can assist individuals with ASD capability better. For instance, medicine could assist with overseeing high energy levels, failure to concentrate, or self-hurting conduct, for example, head banging or hand gnawing. Medicine can likewise assist with overseeing co-happening mental circumstances, for example, tension or discouragement, notwithstanding ailments like seizures, rest issues, or stomach or other gastrointestinal issues.

It is critical to work with a specialist who has insight into treating individuals with ASD while thinking about the utilization of prescriptions. This applies to both physician-endorsed prescription and non-prescription medicine. People, families, and specialists should cooperate to screen progress and responses to be certain that pessimistic results of the prescription don't offset the advantages.

Mental Approaches

Mental methodologies can assist individuals with ASD to adapt to uneasiness, gloom, and other emotional well-being issues. Mental Behavior Therapy (CBT) is one mental methodology that spotlights learning the associations between considerations, sentiments, and ways of behaving. During CBT, a specialist and the singular work together to recognize objectives and afterward change the individual's opinion on a circumstance to change how they respond to the circumstance.

Corresponding and Alternative Treatments

A few people and guardians use medicines that don't squeeze into any of the different classes. These medicines are known as Complementary and Alternative medicines. Correlative and elective medicines are in many cases used to enhance more conventional methodologies. They could incorporate extraordinary weight control plans, homegrown supplements, chiropractic care, creature treatment, expressions treatment, care, or unwinding treatments. People and families ought to constantly converse with their PCP prior to beginning a corresponding and elective treatment.

There might be different medicines accessible for people with ASD. Converse with a specialist or medical care supplier to find out more.

Section three

Chapter four

A simple routine for effective management of Autism

While there is no "fix" for mental imbalance, there are a few compelling intercessions that can further develop a kid's working:

Applied conduct examination: It includes precise investigation of the kid's practical difficulties, which is utilized to make an organized social arrangement for working on their versatile abilities and diminishing improper way of behaving

Interactive abilities preparing: Done in gathering or individual settings, this mediation assists youngsters with chemical imbalance work on their capacity to explore social circumstances

Discourse and language treatment: It can further develop the kid's discourse examples and comprehension of language
Word-related treatment: This address versatile abilities deficiencies with exercises of everyday living, as well as issues with penmanship

Parent the board preparing: Parents learn viable approaches to answering tricky ways of behaving and empowering proper conduct in their kids. Parent support bunches assist guardians with adapting to the stressors of bringing up a youngster with a mental imbalance

Custom curriculum administrations: Under an Individual Education Plan given by their school, which obliges for their social correspondence deficiencies, limited interests, and dreary ways of behaving, youngsters with mental imbalance can accomplish their fullest potential scholastically. This incorporates exceptional day classes for extremely small kids to address language, social, and fundamental abilities.

Treating co-happening conditions: Children with mental imbalance experience sleep deprivation, tension, and discouragement more frequently than peers without mental imbalance. They more frequently have ADHD. Kids with mental imbalance might have a scholarly handicap and this should be tended to. The effect of these circumstances can be diminished with the appropriate administrations, which incorporate all of the abovementioned, likewise psychotherapy or potentially medical treatment

Drug: A kid specialist can assess for co-dismal sorrow, uneasiness, and impulsivity. On the off chance that proper prescriptions can be useful. For instance, mental imbalance-related crabbiness can be diminished by prescriptions, for example, aripiprazole and risperidone (the two meds endorsed by the Food and Drug Administration for peevishness related to chemical imbalance), recommended reasonably by a proficient clinician as a team with the kid's folks.

10 Easy-to-Implement Behavior Strategies for kids

Working with youngsters with mental imbalance can be testing and furthermore very fulfilling. Every single day represents another experience in advancing as well as in conduct. Instructors, paraprofessionals, and guardians who work with youngsters with chemical imbalance should be ready with a tool kit of methodologies and strategies to make their lives more straightforward as well as to assist their kids with finding true success and gaining the mediation they deserve.

There are 10 social procedures that are really simple to execute with kids with a chemical imbalance, in the study hall and even at home.

1. Keep pursuing to find out about the accompanying… Show using time effectively
2. Set reasonable assumptions
3. Support positive ways of behaving
4. Give decisions for non-favored exercises
5. Use visuals and social stories
6. Show adapting abilities and quieting techniques
7. Practice changes
8. Be steady every day
9. Think about tactile requirements
10. Show self-observing and feeling guideline

1. Show Time Management

Show Time ManagementChildren with mental imbalance frequently struggles with dealing with their time, for example, understanding how long it requires to finish a movement. An illustration of this is an educator permitting ten minutes for recess until the following movement starts. In the event that the youngster knows nothing about precisely how long they have left, recess might end unexpectedly and make them respond adversely. Utilizing a sand clock or a visual clock will assist teachers with effectively conveying how long is left for specific exercises. Being proactive with clocks and updating with understudies with mental imbalance will assist with diminishing issue ways of behaving while likewise showing the understudies how to self-oversee time and to contemplate advances.

2. Set Realistic Expectations

All kids benefit from rules, systems, and assumptions, and youngsters with a chemical imbalance in all actuality do so significantly more because of their handicap and the way that they need more design and consistency than the typical kid. Setting reasonable assumptions implies thinking about the entire youngster and deciding customized methodology and decisions in light of that specific understudy's requirements. Few out of every odd kid is something similar; side effects of chemical imbalance are on a range, and that implies the necessities will be different for every kid.

The following are 4 hints on setting reasonable assumptions from Autism Classroom Resources:

- Make them certain
- Have understudies assist with making them
- Establish assumptions for every climate/action
- Attach assumptions to a support framework

An illustration of a reasonable assumption for a rudimentary understudy who meanders the homeroom when they enter the class.

3. Support Positive Behaviors

Very much like conduct assumptions should be clarified to the youngsters in a homeroom, it is likewise similarly vital to support suitable ways of behaving, like following assumptions emphatically. It may very well be helpful for kids with a chemical imbalance to know about what they are really going after, for example, 5 free minutes on a PC game, additional break time, or a piece of chocolate. Youngsters can likewise have something to do with what they are really going after; this will guarantee that the support will truly be building up. For instance, giving spare energy on a PC to nothing about understudying innovation and would prefer to go swing on the swingset outside, will be less spurred to consent on the off chance that they realize they will procure something they aren't keen on.

A couple of significant interesting points while picking and furnishing fortifications to youngsters with chemical imbalance are…

Get with the kid and do a support stock to decide different preferences.
Before every action, assist the kid with concluding what they are really going after.
Place a visual close to the youngster to help them to remember what they are really going after.
Be reliable; assuming the youngster finishes the assumptions, they should be given support.
On the off chance that a reinforcer does not work anymore, have a go at something different!
Utilizing encouraging feedback is a magnificent and basic method for altering conduct… use it for your potential benefit at home and in the study hall with your youngsters with a chemical imbalance.

4. Give Choices For Non-Preferred Activities
Giving Choices For Non-Preferred Activities is significant for any kid to have a feeling of control.

Giving youngsters straightforward decisions to make, permits them to feel included and enabled. Make certain to give unmistakable decisions as youngsters with chemical imbalance might be overpowered by such a large number of choices. For instance, inquiring as to whether they'd favor squeezed orange over grape juice or on the other hand on the off chance that they might want to play a game over watching a film ought to be fine. On the off chance that a youngster experiences issues with language, make certain to have clear lines of sight of the choices so they can choose without anyone else.

Decision-making can be utilized over the course of the day, from what movement to begin with, what sort of reinforcer to pursue, or on the other hand assuming they favor composing or verbally expressing their response. The simplest method for utilizing decisions with kids with chemical imbalance is by utilizing a visual decision board that shows pre-chosen choices for the circumstance and has the understudy highlight or say which choice they would like.

In general, permitting youngsters to settle on decisions at school and at home advantages all interested parties and assists with inspiration and consistency.

5. Use Visuals and Social Stories

A decision board is a great illustration of a visual. Numerous kids with chemical imbalance need visual updates, prompts, and social stories over the course of the day to keep focused and find lasting success. Involving an assortment of visuals such as pictures, flip outlines, banners, and cards assists with supporting understudies' requirements. They are utilized to plan understudies for changes, to assist with deciding, to give them answer choices to questions, and so on.

Social stories, specifically, are utilized to get ready kids with chemical imbalance for impending occasions or for changes. A few stories are just basic sentences while others consolidate numerous visuals for non-perusers. An illustration of a circumstance where an understudy could require a social story is in the event that little Johnny frequently has issues with ways of behaving just before the time has come to get on the school transport by the day's end. His instructor makes a social story with visuals to peruse with him once he tidies his region up for the

afternoon and is trusting that his transport will be called. It comprises four straightforward sentences and depicts why Johnny should get on the transport and the means he should take to make it there. Johnny and his instructor will keep on pursuing his social story every day, then occasionally after once issue ways of behaving have stopped.
There are countless pre-made social stories online for a wide range of circumstances and the website Your Therapy Source guides people through making their own without any preparation.

6. Show Coping Skills and Calming Strategies
Show Coping Skills and Calming StrategiesChildren with chemical imbalance totally should be shown adapting abilities and quieting procedures for when they are feeling disappointed, restless, or are having tactile over-burden. For lower-level ASD understudies, they might require help with utilizing these systems and won't have the option to freely do them. It is entirely expected for kids with a chemical imbalance to appear to be restless, squirm, or even have an implosion. Giving physical and close-to-home devices to assist with quieting the body and psyche is significant during seasons of pressure or tangible over-burden.

Instances of these incorporate giving a weighted cover, a fun seat, a squirm or other tactile toy to play with, turning the lights down, playing delicate music, giving commotion dropping earphones to wear, and permitting the understudy to utilize a tangible room or go to a quiet space in the study hall, rehearsing profound breathing and extending, counting in reverse, tapping, and so on. Every kid will have their own inclinations and what is utilized will likewise rely on the circumstance. A SPED instructor and a parent of a youngster with mental imbalance ought to have a "tool stash" loaded with quieting procedures helpful.

7. Practice Transitions

Youngsters with mental imbalance frequently struggle with progressing starting with one spot or action and then onto the next. This is on the grounds that a few people with mental imbalance have inflexible reasoning, struggle with multi-step headings, and have mental moves that assist them with doing specific things freely and effortlessly. Leader working is essential during the shift between activity to activity a great deal is happening in the mind during this time. Educators and guardians can work on progressing with kids with a chemical imbalance in extraordinary ways so they are more ready and ready to adapt to the regular changes.

An article in Psychology Today shares five methodologies that can be utilized to assist kids with a mental imbalance to handle advances well are:

- Give early notification before progress will happen
- Utilize visual backings
- Use design and consistency
- Utilize decreased language
- Give light commendation to great changes

Being proactive while managing advances and expressly rehearsing them with kids with chemical imbalance will assist things with going considerably more easily.

8. Be Consistent Each Day

Consistency is critical! Youngsters with chemical imbalance blossom with consistent examples and a dependable timetable. Switching around their schedules over the course of the day, from one day to another, isn't encouraged. Giving a kid with chemical imbalance a visual timetable for their day and staying on track can help them in being free, in getting ready for changes and what is coming up next in their day, and diminishes uneasiness and stress. Kids on the range will generally favor rules and routine over suddenness and taking the path of least resistance. Instructors and guardians of these kids will realize rapidly that being conflicting isn't what is ideal. Obviously, things happen that are beyond their control; in those occurrences, it is in every case great to understand what the quieting procedures are and furthermore the thing Plan B will be.

9. Think about Sensory Needs

There are different justifications for why a kid with mental imbalance could have tangible issues. They might be delicate to light or sounds, they could have delicate skin and have areas of strength for a for just delicate textures without labels, they probably won't care for different youngsters in that frame of mind to them, or they could have abhorrences, for example, a homeroom entryway being open or strolling down the foyer with different classes about.

While some of the time grown-ups should limit the openness that their youngsters have to their tactile triggers, some may really believe should do the inverse and open them to these things to prepare them to acknowledge them. For example, assuming that an understudy becomes forceful when s/he hears someone else cry (at school, home, and local area), that risky conduct should be tended to, as hearing somebody cry is something that could occur without warning, in any climate, and isn't something anybody has some control over.

Regardless of those circumstances, kids with chemical imbalance ought to be given tactile necessities to assist them with adapting to their surroundings.

10. Show Self-Monitoring and Emotion Regulation

Ultimately, self-checking actual feelings and having the option to direct those feelings is significant expertise for kids with a chemical imbalance to learn. Indeed, even a few kids who are non-verbal can show how they feel somehow and express their necessities. Youngsters in school and at the home can be shown how to screen their own way of behaving and feeling.

This is handily finished by making a diagram or visual or some likeness in the homeroom, for example, an understudy with a chemical imbalance can highlight an image with a furious face in the event that they are upset or flip over a red card to the flag they need a break. Utilizing count graphs, timetables, and pictures are well-known ways of assisting youngsters with turning out to be freer in observing their ways of behaving and sentiments.

Roles of parenting

By and large, guardians assume a significant part in any youngster's life until they arrive at adulthood. In any case, with regards to the children determined to have Autism, in this situation, the guardians' job turns out to be more urgent. To help their kid to adapt to the problem. Guardians need to assume various parts like an instructor, specialist, etc. Simultaneously, guardians will be unable to focus on different children in the family. As they concentrate on the youngster with the issue which requires some investment and energy.

Other than these adverse consequences, many guardians make a point to carry an uplifting tone into the family by keeping the adverse consequences under control. Guardians of Autism kids, by and large, will be under gigantic pressure by going to the requirements of the youngster. The main thing they neglect is dealing with themselves. Remaining solid and positive is dependably fitting.

With regards to the youngster with Autism problems taking them out to play or blend with individuals is an extremely challenging errand since it is moving them from their usual range of familiarity. In any case, guardians should ensure that despite the fact that they are depleted they need to take their children out for their satisfaction and prosperity. Make them attempt new things so they can adapt to changes throughout everyday life.

Join a parent bunch like yours or enlist yourself in the Special kid actual preparation exercises in your space. Collaboration with different guardians who have a comparable youngster like your aides you a great deal to grasp the issue in a superior manner. Indeed, even the youngster feels improved while collaborating with a comparative confused kid. On the other hand, one might in fact demand an Advocate at the IEP meeting whenever required. It is one most effective way to watch out for the Autism kid in school to have a superior improvement. Likewise, guardians need not stress over the youngster in school.

Chapter five

Why do kids with Autism experience issues learning in a standard homeroom setting

There are many reasons that a youngster determined to have mental imbalance range problems can't learn in a customary study hall setting. These incorporate however are not restricted to the accompanying reasons:

- existing together learning handicaps.
- coinciding scholarly inability.
- discourse and correspondence delays.
- animosity to self or others.
- full of feeling Instability.
- require individual oversight to take part in the study hall.
- social correspondence issues.

Subsequently, exceptional endeavors should be made by guardians and parental figures to investigate choices so the kid's capacities are boosted. Accessibility of assets contrasts by local area so it means a lot to contact a kid and juvenile specialist or pediatrician to examine the choices accessible locally.

The ideal ways to teach kids with Autism Spectrum

The quantity of children with mental imbalance is on the ascent. So a profound comprehension of the systems and interactive abilities expected to deal with a class of medically introverted youngsters is critical.

Recorded are a few dependable systems that will guarantee each mentally unbalanced youngster gets the best.

These techniques apply to both the study hall and home conditions.

Design or routine is the situation with regards to chemical imbalance. Keep up with a similar everyday daily schedule, just making exemptions for exceptional events. During such minutes, place a particular picture that portrays the day's occasions in the youngster's very own organizer.

Plan a climate liberated from invigorating variables:

a. Try not to play clearly ambient sound as it makes it challenging for the medically introverted kid to think.

b. Dispose of pressure in light of the fact that mentally unbalanced kids rapidly get on pessimistic feelings. So for instance, on the off chance that you're encountering an excessive amount of pressure, leave the homeroom until you feel much improved.

c. Keep a low and unmistakable voice while drawing in the class. Understudies with mental imbalance get effectively unsettled and confounded in the event that a talking voice is excessively clear.

d. A few medically introverted individuals find glaring lights diverting on the grounds that they can see the glimmer of the 60-cycle power. To alleviate this impact:

Place the kid's work area close to the window or attempt to try not to utilize glaring lights out and out.

In the event that the lights are undeniable, utilize the most up-to-date bulbs you have as they glimmer less.
You can likewise put a light with a dated glowing light close to the kid's work area.

e. Allow understudies to remain as opposed to lounging around a table for a class show or during morning and night gatherings. Numerous understudies with mental imbalance will more often than not rock to and fro so standing permits them to rehash those developments while as yet paying attention to the instructor.
Keep verbal directions short and forthright, on the grounds that a mentally unbalanced understudy might find it hard to review the whole grouping. All things being equal, record the guidelines on a piece of paper.

Go for dull movements while chipping away at projects. For instance, most medically introverted study halls have a region for workbox errands, like taking care of erasers and pencils. This sort of consistency assists medically introverted messes with remaining coordinated.

Use signs, pictures, and shows for visual students. For instance:

a. While showing all over developments, connect cards with the words "up" and "down" to a toy plane. The "up" card is appended when the plane takes off while the "down" card is joined when it lands.
b. Utilize a wooden apple cut up into four pieces and a wooden pear cut down in the middle to assist understudies with chemical imbalance grasp the idea of quarters and parts.

"I think in pictures. I don't think in language. The sum total of my viewpoints resembles tapes running in my creative mind. Pictures are my most memorable language."

A few assertions you can recount on troublesome days

"Building a relationship with mentally unbalanced kids doesn't work out coincidentally — it requires investment, devotion, and tolerance."

"Each error I make is significant criticism for sorting out what works."

"I will not necessarily in all occasions get things without taking a beating and, at last, mentally unbalanced youngsters are still kids, who can be a small bunch even in the most ideal circumstances."

"Mentally unbalanced youngsters aren't troublesome deliberately. They're just doing all that can be expected with their perspective and accessible help."

"Great educators assisted me with making progress. I had the option to defeat mental imbalance since I had great educators. At age 2 1/2 I was put in an organized nursery school with experienced educators. Kids with mental imbalance need to have an organized day and educators who realize that generally will be firm yet delicate."

How to handle furious autistic kids

- What to do during an exceptionally boisterous, extremely open implosion

- Be sympathetic: Sympathy implies tuning in and recognizing their battle without judgment. ...
- Cause them to have a good sense of reassurance and cherish it. ...
- Dispose of disciplines. ...
- Center around your youngster, not gazing at spectators. ...
- Break out your tactile toolbox. …
- Show them survival techniques once they're quiet

Risk factors

The quantity of kids determined to have mental imbalance range jumble is rising. It's not satisfactory whether this is because of a better location and revealing or a genuine expansion in the number of cases, or both.
Mental imbalance range jumble influences offspring of all races and identities, however certain variables increment a youngster's gamble. These may include:

Your kid's sex: Young men are multiple times bound to foster chemical imbalance range jumble than young ladies are.

Family ancestry: Families who have one youngster with mental imbalance range jumble have an expanded gamble of having one more kid with the problem. It's likewise normal for guardians or family members of a kid with chemical imbalance range turmoil to generally dislike social or relational abilities themselves or to participate in specific ways of behaving common of the issue.

Different issues: Kids with specific ailments have a higher than the typical gamble of chemical imbalance range confusion or chemical imbalance like side effects. Models incorporate delicate X disorder, an acquired issue that creates scholarly issues; tuberous sclerosis, a condition in which harmless cancers foster in the cerebrum; and Rett disorder, a hereditary condition happening only in young ladies, which causes easing back of head development, scholarly inability and loss of deliberate hand use.

Very preterm children: Children brought into the world before 26 weeks of growth might have a more serious gamble of chemical imbalance range jumble.

Guardians' ages. There might be an association between kids brought into the world to more established guardians and chemical imbalance range jumble, yet more exploration is important to lay out this connection.

Difficulties

Issues with social associations, correspondence, and conduct can prompt:

Issues in school and with fruitful learning

Business issues

Failure to autonomously live

Social confinement

Stress inside the family

Exploitation and being tormented

Conclusion

Finding out about and understanding the way of behaving and techniques for dealing with youngsters with mental imbalance is the initial step all educators and guardians who work with this populace ought to take. These techniques don't need a lot of exertion and they are regular things that guardians and educators do at any rate and don't for a moment even understand that they are carrying out a genuine ABA conduct methodology. The primary things to recollect are to be predictable, carry out them accurately, and on the off chance that something isn't working, take a stab at something different or change how you are getting things done. Working with kids who have mental imbalance while changing ways of behaving has a ton to do with experimentation. You need to keep attempting techniques to see what turns out best for every individual kid, as no kid is indistinguishable.

It's absolutely impossible to forestall mental imbalance range jumble, however, there are treatment choices. Early finding and mediation are generally useful and can further develop conduct, abilities, and language advancement.

Notwithstanding, intercession is useful at whatever stage in life. However, youngsters ordinarily don't grow out of mental imbalance range jumble side effects, they might figure out how to work well.

www.ingramcontent.com/pod-product-compliance
Lightning Source LLC
LaVergne TN
LVHW050345160826
845677LV00014B/3797

* 9 7 9 8 8 4 6 8 6 5 6 3 1 *